Contents

Introduction   6

Journey map   8

On the forest floor   10

The buttress roots   12

The understorey   14

The tree at night   16

Towards the light   18

The crowded canopy   20

The emergent layer   22

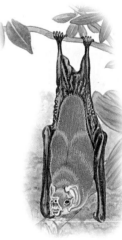

AMAZING JOURNEYS

Up a Rainforest Tree

Carole Telford and Rod Theodorou

www.heinemann.co.uk/library
Visit our website to find out more information about Heinemann Library books.

To order:
☎ Phone 44 (0) 1865 888112
📄 Send a fax to 44 (0) 1865 314091
💻 Visit the Heinemann bookshop at www.heinemann.co.uk/library to browse our catalogue and order online.

First published in Great Britain by Heinemann Library, Halley Court, Jordan Hill, Oxford OX2 8EJ, part of Harcourt Education.
Heinemann is a registered trademark of Harcourt Education Ltd.

© Harcourt Education Ltd 1997, 2006

Editorial: Clare Lewis
Design: Victoria Bevan, Michelle Lisseter, and Bridge Creative Services
Illustrations: Stephen Lings and Jane Pickering at Linden Artists
Picture Research: Hannah Taylor
Production: Helen McCreath

Printed and bound in China by WKT

10 digit ISBN 0 431 05650 1
13 digit ISBN 978 0 431 05650 0

10 09 08 07 06
10 9 8 7 6 5 4 3 2 1

British Library Cataloguing in Publication Data
Theodorou, Rod and Telford, Carole
Amazing journeys: Up a rainforest tree – 2nd edition
577.3'4
A full catalogue record for this book is available from the British Library.

Acknowledgements
The publishers would like to thank the following for permission to reproduce photographs:
Ardea London Ltd. (John S. Dunning) p. **11** (top), (Nick Gordon) p.**14**; Bruce Coleman Limited (Jorg and Petra Wegner) p. **13** (bottom), (Staffan Widstrand) p. **6**, (Dr Eckhart Pott) p. **25** (top), (Gunter Ziesler) p. **17** (bottom); FLPA (Roger Wilmshurst) p. **21** (top); NHPA (Elizabeth MacAndrew) p. **18**, (Haroldo Pala) p. **11** (bottom), Jany Sauvanet) pp. **13** (top), **23** (bottom), **27**, (Martin Wendler) p. **26**; Oxford Scientific Films (Michael Fogden) pp. **17** (top), **19** (top), **21** (bottom), **24**, (Paul Franklin) p. **12**, Richard Packwood) p. **15** (bottom), (P. and W. Ward) p. **15** (top).
Opposite: Oxford Scientific Films.

Cover photograph of a black-handed spider monkey, reproduced with permission of FLPA/ Foto Natura/Flip De Nooyer.

Every effort has been made to contact copyright holders of any material reproduced in this book. Any omissions will be rectified in subsequent printings if notice is given to the publishers.

The paper used to print this book comes from sustainable resources.

At the tree top   **24**

Conservation and the future   **26**

Glossary   **28**

Find out more   **30**

Index   **32**

Some words in the text are bold, **like this**. You can find out what these words mean by looking in the Glossary.

Introduction

You are about to go on an amazing journey.
You are going to travel to one of the most special places in the world: the Amazon **rainforest**.
This is home to one in five of all **species** of plants and half of all species of birds in the world!
You will cross the dark, gloomy floor of the forest and then travel up the mighty trunk of a rainforest tree. You will discover how each part of the tree is home to different kinds of plants and animals.
Each animal has its own special way to move, feed, and **breed** in this amazing world of trees.

Thousands of species of trees, plants, and animals live in this rich **habitat**, which is as hot and **humid** as a greenhouse.

Tropical rainforests grow in areas of the world which are hot but also have a lot of rain. The Amazon rainforest is the largest rainforest in the world. It covers an area about two thirds the size of the United States of America. It is also one of the wettest areas in the world. Two-thirds of the Earth's fresh water can be found here! There are no **seasons**; it is always very hot and very wet.

The Amazon rainforest grows around the mighty River Amazon in South America.

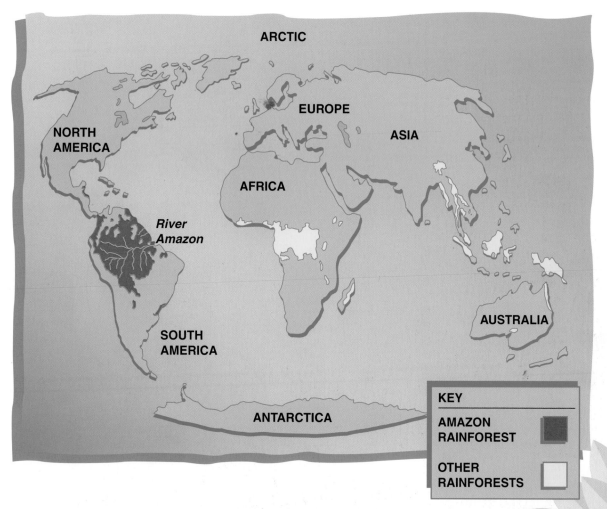

ARCTIC

EUROPE

NORTH AMERICA

ASIA

AFRICA

River Amazon

SOUTH AMERICA

AUSTRALIA

ANTARCTICA

KEY

AMAZON RAINFOREST

OTHER RAINFORESTS

Journey map

This map shows the **rainforest** tree we are going to climb. You can see that each section of the rainforest has a name. We are going to start on the forest floor and climb slowly up towards the **canopy** high above us. Only a few very tall trees, called **emergents**, manage to grow above the canopy. A tree this tall takes a long time to grow. It may be as much as 100 years old!

30 Metres

Metres

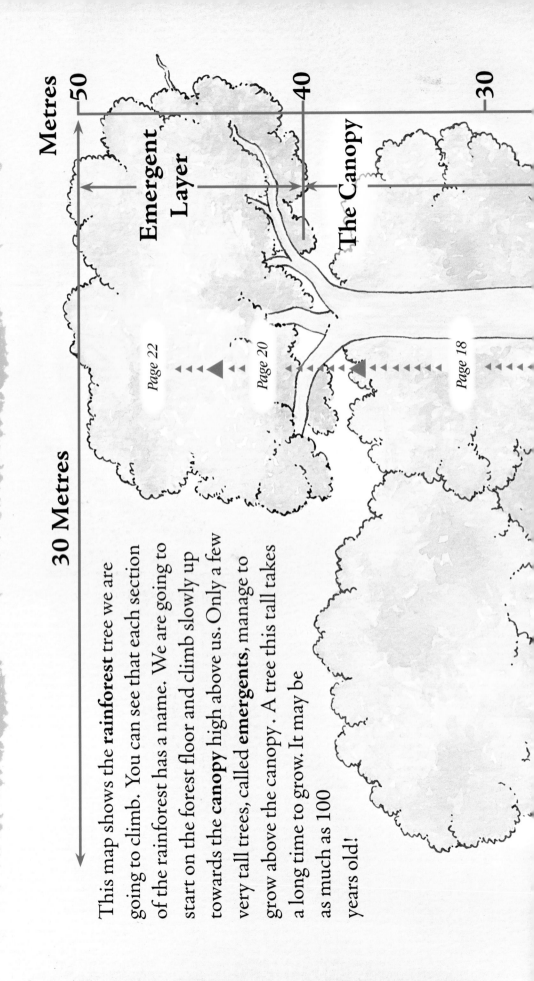

Emergent Layer

The Canopy

50

40

30

Page 22

Page 20

Page 18

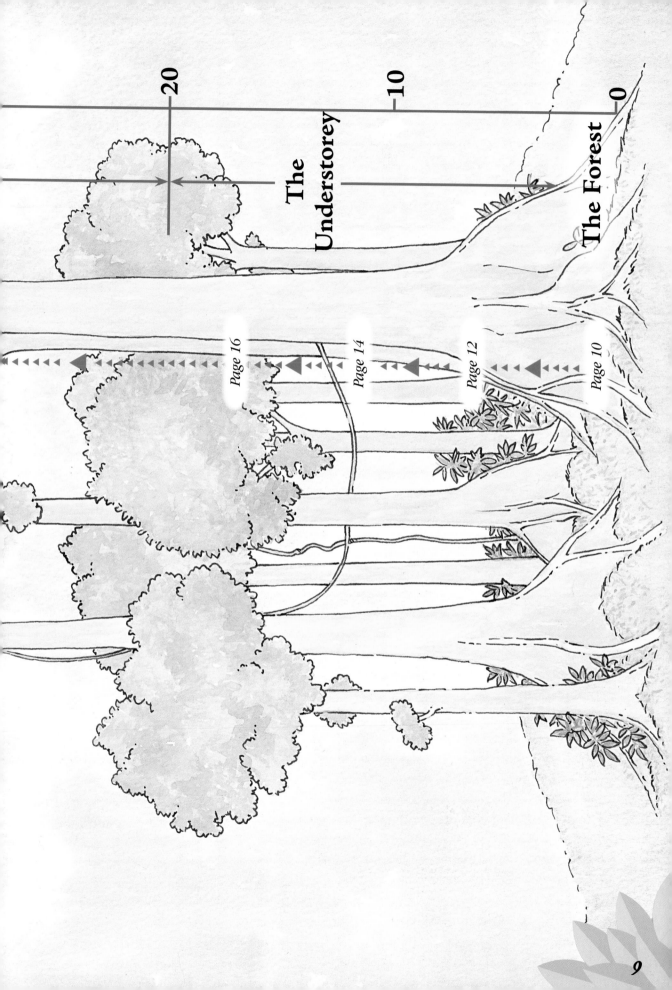

20

10

0

The Understorey

The Forest

Page 16

Page 14

Page 12

Page 10

9

On the forest floor

We are walking through the **rainforest**. The air is full of the call of birds and the buzz of insects. The air is **humid**, like in a hot steamy shower. Even though it is daytime it is quite dark. High above us the thick **canopy** of leaves blocks out nearly all the sunlight. It is too dark for grass to grow. Instead the ground under our feet is thick with twigs and dead leaves that have fallen from above. Many types of **fungi** grow here, helping to rot the **leaf litter**. The rotting leaves release **nutrients** which trees and plants take up into their roots to help them grow.

Fungi and rotting leaf litter provide food for thousands of tiny creatures such as beetles, ants, and wood lice.

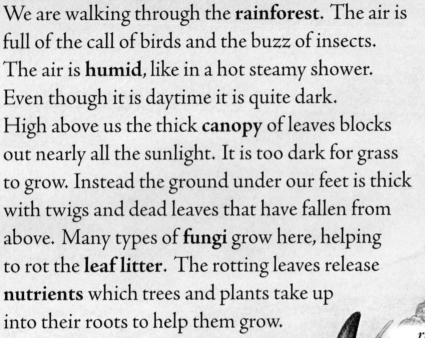

rhinoceros beetle

crab spider

millipede

fungi

seedling

centipede

leaf-cutter ants

army ants

Ant bird

This small forest bird has a special way of feeding. Army ants travel across the forest floor in columns, attacking insects and small animals. The ant bird flies just ahead of the column and snaps up insects as they try to escape the hungry ants.

Six-banded armadillo

The armadillo uses its strong claws to make a burrow to live in, or to dig for tasty worms and insects. Although it is covered in strong bony plates, it can curl up in a ball if attacked.

Rhinoceros beetle

These beetles are huge – as long as an adult's hand! Rhinoceros beetles are sometimes called Hercules beetles. The male uses his amazing horns to **wrestle** another male, trying to throw him over onto his back.

The buttress roots

As we look around in the gloom we see **shrubs**, small trees, and larger tree trunks. Some trees have been able to grow much taller than the others. They have become giants of the forest, stretching their leaves up to the sunlit **canopy**. If we stand next to one of these trees we feel tiny. Not only is it tall, but it also has huge roots. These special **buttress** roots anchor the tree into the **shallow** soil of the forest floor.

Some buttress roots grow up to 5 metres (16 feet) tall.

Cock of the rock

This small brightly coloured bird eats insects and fruit. The cock of the rock lives near the forest floor where it dances and **displays** to other birds.

Coati

The coati has a striped coat which acts as **camouflage**. It uses its long snout to search out grubs and insects. It can also climb to hunt for birds and lizards.

Jaguar

The jaguar is the biggest cat in the **rainforest**. It lives alone and is an excellent climber and swimmer. It hunts fish, small animals such as mice, or large animals such as capybaras and coatis. With its spotted coat it can blend into the shadows and creep up on its **prey**, such as this tapir.

The understorey

Now we are climbing. The understorey is the dark gloomy area below the tree **canopy**. Because of the thick ceiling of trees hardly any wind can blow down here. It is very still and **humid**. We are surrounded by ferns, palms, vines, and creepers, dripping with **moisture**. They can live here because they do not need much light. Among the shadows and splashes of colour we spot lizards scurrying about, searching for food. A spotted ocelot climbs slowly up a creeper, looking for roosting birds.

Young **saplings** grow up in the gloomy understorey towards the light.

14

Lianas

Lianas are climbing plants, called vines, that grow up other plants and trees. Many animals use these vines like ropes or bridges to travel around the forest.

Tarantulas

These huge spiders can grow as large as 26 cm (10 inches) across. They use their huge, poisonous fangs to catch other spiders, insects, frogs, and small lizards. Tarantulas are also called bird-eating spiders, but they only hunt small **roosting** birds or chicks.

Hoatzin

This strange bird nests in trees beside rivers in the **rainforest**. Baby hoatzins have claws on their wings to help them hold on to the nest and twigs. Hoatzins eat leaves which rot in their stomachs, giving off a disgusting, strong smell.

The tree at night

We decide to make camp for the night in a fork in the tree. As the light fades, the **rainforest** comes alive with the sounds of **nocturnal** creatures. In the darkness it is hard to see what is making the noise. The air vibrates with the sound of buzzing cicadas, grasshoppers, and croaking frogs. When we hear one frog croaking we sometimes hear another answering back. A large moth flutters by. We see the shadowy shape of a bat swoop past to catch it.

silky anteater

insect-eating bat

termite nest

fruit bats

ocelot

nectar-sipping bat

Silky anteater

The silky anteater gets its name from its fine, soft coat. It lives all its life among the trees and vines, using its sharp claws and **prehensile** tail to climb. It hunts at night, feeding on ants and termites with its long, thin, sticky tongue.

Margay

This small cat, about 80 cm (30 inches) long, is related to the ocelot. It is a great climber and can leap with ease from branch to branch. Its creamy coat with black spots makes it hard to see as it hunts for birds and small animals.

Fruit bats

Fruit bats are sometimes called flying foxes. They feed on fruit, **nectar**, and **pollen**. Sometimes this pollen gets stuck on their fur and is carried to other flowers. This helps new plants to grow. During the day the bats sleep, hanging from branches.

Towards the light

It has been a long night. As day breaks in the forest we begin our climb further up towards the **canopy**. **Nocturnal** animals are hurrying to find a safe place to spend the daylight hours. Dawn brings a new chorus of birdsong. A large grasshopper-like insect called a katydid freezes in front of us. In an instant it looks exactly like a dead leaf. **Camouflage** is important in the **rainforest**. It protects animals from their enemies and helps them surprise their **prey**. We have to look carefully to spot snakes that look like vines and insects that look like leaves.

In the daylight hours, colour and shape become very important for plants and animals.

Poison arrow frog

This frog does not use camouflage. Its colours are bright and easy to see. They are a warning sign to any **predator**. This frog has a poison in its skin which can kill even large predators such as snakes and monkeys.

Emerald boa

The emerald boa lives among the trees where it uses its colour as camouflage. It can grow up to 2 metres (6.5 feet) in length. It hunts parrots and monkeys, which it squeezes to death in its strong **coils**.

Praying mantis

This mantis is the same colour as the leaves where it hides. It keeps completely still until another insect comes close. Then it uses its fast and powerful front legs to grab its prey.

The crowded canopy

Now we are into the **canopy**. It is less gloomy here and not as **humid**. The leaves and branches are so dense it is hard to climb. All around we can hear birds and monkeys calling out. We can see many different kinds of monkey, using the vines to clamber around us. Beautiful flowers grow here, and the trees are rich with fruit. Parrots and butterflies flash their dazzling colours.

More animals live in the canopy than anywhere else in the rainforest.

toucan

three-toed sloth

macaw

parrot

tamandua

woolly monkey

white-faced capuchin

green whip snake

Morpho butterfly

This large butterfly can measure up to 10 cm (4 inches) across its wings. It feeds on the **nectar** in flowers. The male morpho butterflies are the most brightly coloured to attract a mate. They have special **scales** on their wings which catch the light and shine.

Three-toed sloth

This strange animal always moves very slowly. It hangs from branches all its life with powerful claws like hooks. Its fur is so damp and dirty that green **moss** and **algae** grow there. This helps to hide the sloth from its enemies.

Toucan

Many kinds of toucan live in the **rainforest**. Their long beaks and tongues can reach fruit growing on branches that are too thin to **perch** on. Sometimes they also eat lizards.

The emergent layer

At last we reach sunlight! The **emergent** layer is made up of the tallest, oldest trees in the forest. The blazing hot sun beats down on the tops of smaller trees around us, drying their leaves. It is far less **humid** here. There is even a gentle breeze. Here it is much easier to spot brightly coloured hummingbirds searching for flowers and fruits to feed on. We can also hear the loud whooping calls of howler monkeys.

The rainforest is home to 250 varieties of mammals and 1,800 **species** of birds.

fruit bat

spider monkey

Amazon parrot

blue-headed parrot

bromeliad

iguana

mouse opossum

Howler monkey

These are the largest and loudest monkeys in the **rainforest**. They have a special bone in their throat which acts like a trumpet when they call out. Their calls can be heard for miles, usually at dawn and dusk.

Hummingbird

By flapping their wings very fast, hummingbirds can hover and even fly backwards. They fly quickly from flower to flower amongst the branches, feeding off **nectar** with their long bills.

Gliding tree frog

The gliding tree frog climbs up tall trees and then jumps. Webbed hands and feet act like parachutes, helping it glide to other trees over 12 metres (40 feet) away.

At the tree top

Now we are at the very top of our **rainforest** tree. We are just above the **canopy** on a platform of leaves swaying in the wind. The sun is beating down fiercely. Insects fill the air, chased by **agile** swifts. Around us in the canopy we can see flashes of movement and colour. Sharp-eyed eagles can see them too and are ready to swoop down to snatch a monkey or parrot for a meal.

The view from the very top of the rainforest tree is spectacular!

Scarlet macaw

The rainforest is home to many different kinds of parrots. The scarlet macaw is one of the largest. Like most parrots, it can fly or clamber through the branches and uses its strong beak to crack open nuts and fruit.

Spider monkey

This large monkey is too big to be hunted by eagles. With its long thin legs and tail it looks like a spider crawling through the branches. By drinking **nectar** from flowers spider monkeys help the **pollination** of the forest.

Harpy eagle

The harpy eagle is the largest and most powerful bird in the rainforest. It is a fast and skilful **predator**. It can fly at speeds of up to 80 km/h (50 mph) through the branches to snatch monkeys, or sloths, in its strong **talons**.

Conservation and the future

At the end of our journey we enjoy one of the most wonderful views in the world – a view across the **rainforest** as it stretches in every direction like a vast green carpet. However, we also see smoke in the distance, curling up between the trees. People are destroying the rainforest. Rainforests are being cut down for timber, fuel, or to make room for cattle to feed. Every second an area of the Amazon rainforest the size of a football pitch is destroyed! This is a disaster for our planet.

Rainforests are the richest places on Earth, but every day they are being destroyed.

Why do we need rainforests?

Rainforests have been called the lungs of the Earth. This is because trees in the rainforest release a gas called oxygen which we need to breathe. When lots of trees are cut down there is less oxygen and more gas called carbon dioxide. Too much carbon dioxide could make the earth hotter and cause great damage.

Once a rainforest has been cut down it will never grow again. Tree roots hold the valuable soil in place. Without them the soil washes away. Farmers often use the land for their cattle. The cattle eat the remaining plant life, leaving nothing but dust.

You can help save the rainforests by joining organizations that are working to preserve them. Thousands of **species** of animals need the rainforests to survive. Without these amazing places, it will be the end of their journey for ever.

Rainforest animals such as Humboldt's monkey are already in danger of extinction.

Glossary

agile   can move quickly

algae   very small plants which live in water and damp places

breed   to make more young animals

buttress   to push against and prop up

camouflaged   coloured or shaped in a way that makes an animal hard to see

canopy   the tallest layer of trees in the forest

coils   the rings a snake can form with its body to squeeze its prey

displays   shows off bright coloured feathers

emergent   tree which grows above the canopy towards the light

fungi   soft, spongy plant like a mushroom

habitat   the place in which an animal lives

humid   hot and steamy

leaf litter   rotting leaves and plants which lie on the forest floor

liana   twisting, climbing plant

moisture   makes things wet

moss   type of tiny plant which grows in damp places

nectar   a sweet liquid like honey that some plants make to attract birds, bats, and insects

nocturnal   animal that is active at night and rests during the day

nutrient   substance taken in by plants and animals to help them grow

perch	sit or rest
pollen	tiny yellow grains produced by male parts of plants which fertilize the female parts
pollination	the transfer of pollen from male to female part of a flower, which makes seeds
predator	animal that hunts and kills other animals for food
prehensile	flexible tail which an animal can use to hold on to branches
prey	animal that is caught and eaten by another animal
rainforest	forest in a warm place with heavy rainfall
roosting	sleeping on a perch
sapling	a young tree
scales	the thin flakes that coat the wings of a butterfly
seasons	parts of the year that have different weather
shallow	a thin layer
shrub	low, bushy plant
species	group of living things that are very similar
talon	sharp claw of a hunting bird
wrestle	to hold on to and try to throw down

Find out more

Further reading

Food Chains: Rainforest, Emma Lynch (Heinemann Library, 2004)

Rainforest (DK Revealed), Jen Green, Mark Longworth (Dorling Kindersley, 2004)

The Vanishing Rainforest, Richard Platt, Rupert Van Wyk (Frances Lincoln, 2003)

Organizations

Coral Cay Conservation

40–42 Osnaburgh Street

London

NW1 3ND

www.coralcay.org

Rainforest Foundation

City Cloisters

196 Old Street

London EC1V 9FR

www.rainforestfoundationuk.org

Using the Internet

If you want to find out more about rainforests, you can go to one of the website addresses below. Alternatively, you can use a search engine, such as www.yahooligans.com or www.internet4kids.com, and type in a keyword such as "rainforest", or a related subject such as "scarlet macaw".

Websites

www.panda.org

This is the WWF website – click on "Forests" for news about the rainforest.

www.enchantedlearning.com/subjects/rainforest/animals/

This site provides information and print-outs on rainforest animals.

http://www.rainforestfoundationuk.org

The Rainforest Foundation works for the preservation of the forests, and its website includes a "Kid's corner".

Index

ant bird 11

army ants 11

buttress roots 12

camouflage 13, 18

canopy 8, 10, 12, 14, 20, 24

cicada 16

coati 13

cock of the rock 13

conservation 26, 27

emerald boa 19

emergent 8

fruit bat 17

fungi 10

gliding tree frog 23

harpy eagle 25

hoatzin 15

howler monkey 22, 23

humboldts monkey 27

hummingbird 23

jaguar 13

leaf litter 10

lianas 15

margay 17

morpho butterfly 21

nocturnal 16, 18

nutrients 10

poison arrow frog 19

praying mantis 19

rhinoceros beetle 11

scarlet macaw 25

silky anteater 17

six-banded armadillo 11

spider monkey 25

tapir 13

tarantula 15

three-toed sloth 21

toucan 20, 21

understorey 14